Birds
Brilliant & Bizarre

Joanne Cooper

Published by the Natural History Museum, London

Contents

Foreword

Beccy Speight
Chief Executive, RSPB

Watching swifts screaming high over my garden and the house sparrows chirping merrily in the hedge, it is hard to imagine that these are the modern, living descendants of dinosaurs. While an infamous asteroid is thought to have wiped out most dinosaurs some 66 million years ago, some made it through. The early birds came from the theropod group of dinosaurs and, in various odd leaps and bounds of evolution, modern birds slowly emerged.

The differences between those late dinosaurs, and what would become the birds, are small and blurred. The birds we see today have had to adapt and evolve over millions of years to a changing world. They are extraordinary. In the air, young swifts may fly for four years without touching land, and in the oceans, Emperor Penguins can dive up to 500 metres (1,640 feet) underwater to catch krill.

But as inspiring as this tale is, can the birds keep pace with the man-made changes and threats they face today? The scale and pace of change is alarming, both in terms of biodiversity loss and accelerating climate change. Looking back over the last 50 years in the UK, so much has altered so quickly. There have been some great victories for birds and nature conservation, but those are set against a backcloth of overall continued loss and degradation. The threats are growing not shrinking – from intensive agriculture, the impacts of climate change, pollution, burgeoning development leading to habitat loss, food scarcity and new wildlife diseases, to name just a few. In the UK alone, 38 million birds have vanished from our skies. Whether our birds can adapt to such challenges remains to be seen, but the current signs are not encouraging. They will need all the help we can give them.

This wonderful exhibition is a chance for the RSPB to celebrate our relationship with the Natural History Museum, London and our common vision of a future where nature and people thrive, side by

Spending most of their lives in flight, Common Swifts, *Apus apus,* have long, narrow wings and highly streamlined bodies to generate lift whilst using as little energy as possible.

side. We collaborate on science such as the regular *State of Nature* report – an assessment of how nature is doing in the UK – and on projects around the world, seeking to understand the threats to biodiversity and find the solutions.

Through this partnership, I hope that many people learn more about the exciting story of birds and feel motivated to help ensure these incredible species are around for generations to come. Anyone inspired by what they have seen has the power to act. What you buy, what you eat, where you invest your money, the influence you could have in your local community, how you use your voice, and how you manage your garden or balcony, if you are lucky enough to have one, all matter. Nature is in crisis, but together, we believe, we can save it.

After diving to great depths, Emperor Penguins, *Aptenodytes forsteri,* can release tiny air bubbles, still trapped in their feathers, to help speed up their return to the surface for a swift exit onto the ice.

Surviving catastrophe

Daniel J. Field

Birds are unmistakable among living animals, exhibiting a combination of features unseen anywhere else in nature – a hollow skeleton, a toothless beak and a capacity for flight on feathered wings among a host of other characteristics. But understanding the evolutionary origins of these attributes is challenging and necessitates investigation of the fossil record. Close examination of the features that make birds so distinctive reveals that these characteristics arose at various points during the evolutionary history of long-extinct dinosaurs. Indeed, over the last thirty years, the realization that birds *are* in fact a surviving lineage of unusually small dinosaurs has gained virtually universal acceptance within the scientific community.

Specifically, birds are a highly specialized lineage of a group of dinosaurs called theropods – the group of three-toed, meat-eating dinosaurs that includes such famous representatives as *Tyrannosaurus* and *Velociraptor*. Evidence from recent palaeontological investigations suggests that many specialized 'bird-like' features, like feathers, the ability to walk on two legs, hollow bones, a wishbone and a warm-blooded physiology, would have already existed in *T. rex* and *Velociraptor* and, rather than being intrinsically bird-like, instead represent features that early birds would have inherited from their non-avian theropod ancestors. By contrast, other features such as powered flight, a

With their long tail and similar body size, reconstructions of *Archaeopteryx* often resemble a Eurasian magpie, *Pica pica*. Analysis of an isolated wing feather has revealed that it did indeed have some black plumage, but its complete body pattern remains unknown.

toothless beak and a greatly expanded brain arose later in bird evolutionary history, after the lineages leading to *T. rex* and *Velociraptor* had diverged from the line leading to birds.

Certain fossils have proven to be especially useful for clarifying our understanding of how and when 'bird-like' features first arose. For instance, the 150-million-year-old *Archaeopteryx* has long been considered an evolutionary Rosetta Stone for its combination of ancestral 'dinosaur-like' and derived 'bird-like' features. *Archaeopteryx* combines ancestral features such as a long bony tail, strongly clawed hands and jaws full of sharp teeth with features extremely similar to those we see in living birds: large, feathered wings, asymmetrical flight feathers with a narrow leading edge and a broad trailing edge, and an elongated and reversed hind toe suited for perching on branches. Other remarkable fossils include: *Sinosauropteryx* – a small-bodied theropod dinosaur distantly related to birds that provided the first unambiguous evidence that feathers evolved long before birds; *Microraptor* – a small relative of *Velociraptor* that may have glided with the aid of wings on both its forelimbs and hindlimbs; and *Pengornis*, a representative of an archaic group of birds from the Age of Dinosaurs called enantiornithines, or 'opposite-birds', that appear to have been specialized for life in the trees above the heads of other dinosaurs.

The realization that birds are dinosaurs challenges us to rethink our assumptions about the 'disappearance' of the dinosaurs – these icons of extinction must *not* in fact have completely disappeared in the famed end-Cretaceous mass extinction event 66-million-years ago, when a giant asteroid struck the Earth on the single most devastating day in the history of life on our planet. So, if the early ancestors of modern birds managed to make it through that fateful asteroid impact and its catastrophic aftermath, how did they do it? How could the canaries of the ancient world have been the ones to make it out of that cataclysmic coal mine, when their more robust dinosaurian relatives failed to survive? Avian survivorship across that extinction event would have been by no means assured, especially since all other lineages of dinosaurs, as well as over 70% of all other species on the planet, died out.

Through fossil discoveries in the last decade, such as the 'wonderchicken', *Asteriornis*, palaeontologists have begun to unravel the factors contributing to avian survival in the wake of the asteroid impact. The relatively small size of surviving birds with respect to non-avian dinosaurs would have been beneficial during the impact's scorched aftermath as small-bodied species have lower total energy requirements than large-bodied species, as well as comparatively faster reproductive rates and a capacity for large population sizes; these factors would have favoured small-bodied species once the going got tough. Moreover, although vast numbers of living bird species spend their lives in trees, extinction survivors would have inherited a world virtually

Named after Asteria, the Greek Titan goddess of falling stars, *Asteriornis* is the oldest 'modern bird' fossil ever found. It predates the mass extinction event of 66 million years ago that wiped out the dinosaurs, but its relationship to modern duck-like and chicken-like birds has earned it the nickname 'wonderchicken'.

devoid of forests. The fossil record of plants and pollen suggests that, for a period spanning decades at least and millennia at most, forests were devastated worldwide as a result of impact-associated wildfires and global darkness. Indeed, the bird fossil record fits in with these observations; most archaic bird species from before the asteroid impact were specialized for life in the trees, but these lineages failed to survive through the extinction event. The early ancestors of modern birds that passed through the extinction appear to have been predominantly ground dwelling. Once forests recovered, surviving bird lineages recolonized the treetops – an ecological transition that contributed to their diversification.

In the light of their evolutionary history, the fact that our world is populated by nearly 11,000 species of birds today is simply remarkable. The fossil record attests not only to the amazing evolutionary transition by which birds arose from dinosaurian ancestors, but also to the fact that birds nearly died out along with other dinosaurs 66 million years ago. Viewed through the lens of the fossil record, every living bird is miraculous – even city pigeons!

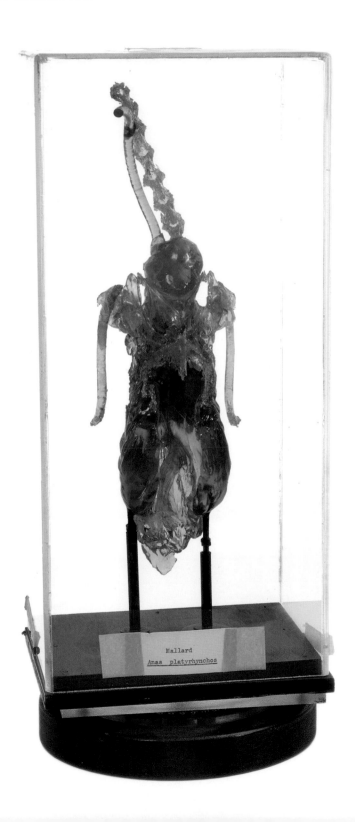

AIR SACS

Mallard air sacs (cast) *Anas platyrhynchos*
Air sac openings in sauropod dinosaur vertebrae
Xenoposeidon proneneukos

Birds have a complex system of air sacs connected to their lungs to help ventilate them. These delicate, walled sacs act as bellows to keep air moving in one direction through the respiratory system, maximizing every oxygen-rich inhalation to fuel the muscles for flight. This cast (opposite) was created by pumping liquid resin into the lungs and air sacs of a dead Mallard duck, then carefully removing everything around the hardened resin. It shows how some of the sacs even extend into parts of the skeleton through small holes called pneumatic foramina. These holes can also be found in dinosaurs (above), revealing that air sacs evolved long before flight.

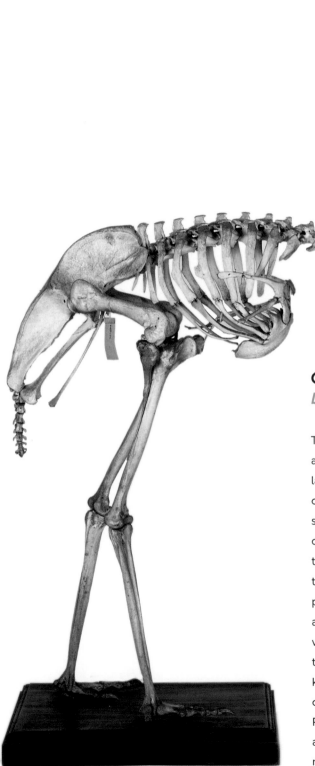

Common Emu
Dromaius novaehollandiae

The oldest known fossils of Common Emu are only about 5 million years old, but these large, flightless birds are descended from one of the earliest known groups of birds that shared the world with their dinosaur relatives over 70 million years ago. Emus show many of the features birds inherited from their distant therapod ancestors: a two-legged bipedal posture, feathers and key bone structures, such as the open back of the hip socket. Together with ostriches, cassowaries, rheas and tinamous, they form a branch of the bird family tree known as the palaeognaths ('old jaws'), which can be traced back to before the Cretaceous–Palaeogene extinction event by fossil remains and DNA analysis of the relationships between modern bird groups.

THEROPODS

Lower jaw *Tyrannosaurus rex*
Skull (cast) *Velociraptor mongoliensis*

The group of three-toed bipedal carnivores known as theropods includes some of the most iconic dinosaurs in the world. Starting in the late 1960s, new discoveries about theropods, their anatomy and lifestyles helped trigger a revolution in our understanding of dinosaurs and consequently birds too. Researchers realized that theropods such as *Velociraptor* and *Tyrannosaurus* must have been active and warm-blooded, not cold-blooded as had been previously thought. This work was made famous by the *Jurassic Park* films

and, from there, a whole new generation of palaeontologists was inspired. Later discoveries revealed even more supposedly bird-like features in the theropods such as evidence of feathers and wishbones. Although some of the ideas were initially controversial, now, after decades of researchers scrutinizing the fossil evidence, it is clear that birds evolved from within the theropods, inheriting a range of characteristic key features before developing unique ones of their own to set them apart.

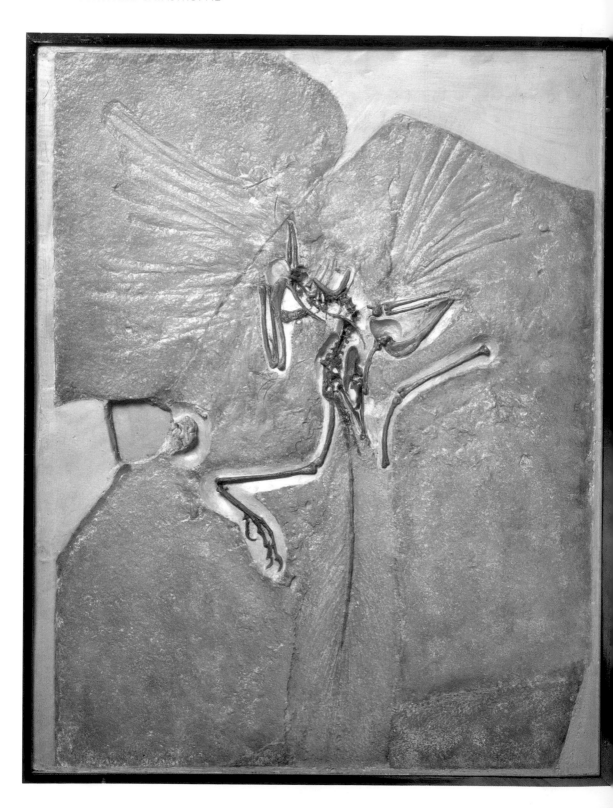

Fossil skeleton
Archaeopteryx lithographica

Discovered in 1861, the specimen at the Natural History Museum, London was the first skeleton of *Archaeopteryx* to be found, making it one of the most important fossils in the world. The limestone slab preserved a small creature with a long, bony tail and teeth like a reptile; but the incredible detail of feather impressions surrounding the skeleton revealed bird-like wings and a plumed tail. The specimen uniquely includes a well-preserved braincase, and researchers were able to carry out a computerized tomography (CT) scan of it to create a virtual reconstruction of *Archaeopteryx'* brain and inner ear. Their analysis showed that *Archaeopteryx* had a bigger brain than an equivalent sized reptile. One-third of the brain was developed for vision, with co-ordination and hearing also important regions. The conclusion was that *Archaeopteryx* had a flight-adapted brain very similar to modern birds, but how well it could fly remains unclear.

Fossil skeleton
Sinosauropteryx prima

Northwestern China has a crucial place in palaeontology as the source region of the Jehol Biota – an extraordinary fossilized record of Early Cretaceous fauna and flora from 133–120 million years ago. Many pivotal discoveries have been made from the Jehol Biota including the exceptionally preserved remains of a small theropod dinosaur with short arms and a very long tail. Described in 1996 and named *Sinosauropteryx prima*, this little dinosaur was only distantly related to birds, but the specimen included impressions of fine filaments around the skeleton, especially along the head, neck, back and down the tail. These proved to be the first evidence of feathers in a non-avian dinosaur, revealing that feathers developed in dinosaurs before birds had evolved. Later analyzes of the feathers of *Sinosauropteryx* found pigment-producing microstructures that revealed the striped pattern along its long tail could have been reddish and white.

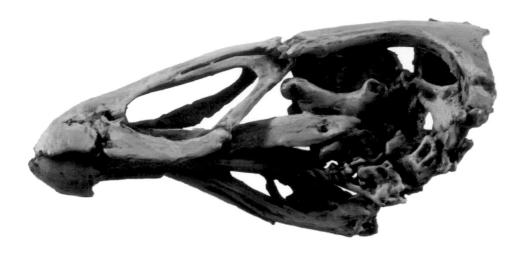

'Wonderchicken'
Asteriornis maastrichtensis

Fossil bird remains are traditionally examined after being taken out of their original rocks or sediments in some way. However, modern techniques such as high-resolution computerized tomography (CT) scanning offer a non-invasive way to examine fragile, inaccessible specimens – with sometimes extraordinary results. Preserved in a small chunk of rock, the remarkable skull of the Late Cretaceous bird *Asteriornis maastrichtensis* was revealed by such scanning. From the virtual model of the skull, which could also be 3D printed, the research team was able to compare their discovery with other fossil and modern birds, including specimens from the Natural History Museum collections. This revealed that the ancient bird shared many features common to the group that includes living chickens and ducks, the Galloanserae. At 66.7 million years old, it is the oldest fossil representative of modern birds and crucial evidence of the ancestral birds that survived the mass extinctions triggered by the catastrophic asteroid strike. Wonderchicken indeed.

Fossil feather
unknown species

Feathers are made of keratin, the tough fibrous protein that also makes hair, hooves, horns and human fingernails strong. Though feathers seem light and delicate they are in fact very resilient and fossilize well if they settle in the right place, often the bottom of a lake. In most of the 50 localities or so worldwide where they are found, where they date between the Late Jurassic and Late Pliocene, the isolated feathers are the only evidence of birds amongst the preserved faunas. The structure of feathers depends on their function, which can help identify where on a bird a fossil feather might have come from, but it is usually impossible to identify the bird itself. This damaged, but otherwise beautifully preserved fossil from the Oligocene (33-23 million years old) deposits of Forcalquier in the Luberon region of France, most closely resembles an outer tail feather.

SHARED ANCESTRAL SURVIVORS

Common Eider (male) *Somateria mollissima*
Sri Lankan Junglefowl (male) *Gallus lafayettii*

Species in the modern bird groups including pheasants and ducks appear very different from each other. However, detailed anatomical analysis, combined with DNA research and the fossil record, reveals the two groups form a single branch of the bird family tree, known as a clade, called the Galloanserae ('Rooster Geese'). This is one of the earliest bird groups known, with the shared ancestors of pheasants and ducks emerging over 70 million years ago, to then survive the Cretaceous–Palaeogene extinction. The two main groups of pheasants and ducks split several million years later and continued to diversify; many extinct fossil species of Galloanserae have been discovered all over the world. Today there are about 470 species in the group, including four species of junglefowl in the pheasant family.

OCEAN GIANTS PAST AND PRESENT

Skull (cast) *Odontopteryx toliapica*
Wandering Albatross skull *Diomedea exulans*

Emerging about 56 million years ago in the Late Palaeocene, an extraordinary but mysterious group of birds dominated ocean skies across the world until only about 2.5 million years ago. These were the Pelagornithidae, commonly known as bony-toothed birds thanks to the rows of tooth-like bony points along their beaks that helped them catch slippery prey like squid. *Odontopteryx toliapica*, from the important Eocene London Clay in Kent, UK, is one of the smallest known species, but its skull – originally including a long straight beak – would have been about the same size as that of the Wandering Albatross, the largest of modern seabirds. *Odontopteryx toliapica* probably had a similar wingspan to large albatrosses at around 3 metres (10 feet), but many pelagornithids were giants with wingspans up to 5-6 metres (16½-19½ feet). They went extinct probably due to major ecological changes in the ocean environment, which they were less able to cope with than more recently evolved seabirds. They represent the fascinating but now lost diversity of birds in the deep past, which we explore hints of today through the fossil record.

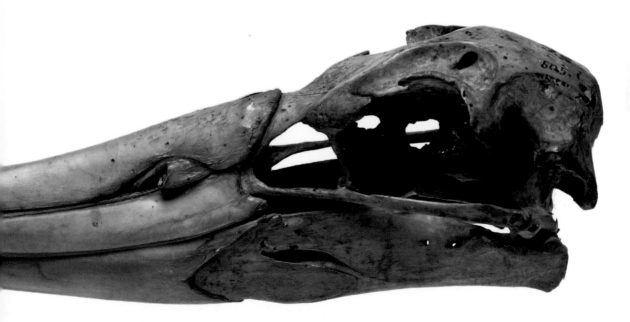

Swift fossil
Scaniacypselus szarskii

A remarkable glimpse of middle Eocene birds,
some 47 million years ago, comes from the
Messel Pit fossil site, southeast of Frankfurt am
Main, Germany where the remains of thousands
of animals and plants have been found. Often
preserved in exquisite detail, the fossils reveal
the inhabitants of an ancient subtropical
forest surrounding a lake. Birds are the most
abundant land vertebrates found here, and 70
species have been identified from large ground
predators to tiny hummingbirds. Amongst the
most rare and beautiful finds is this early swift
with the skeleton surrounded by the striking
impression of its long wings and short tail.
Although apparently a strong acrobatic flier,
Scaniacypselus is thought to have been adapted
for perching and nesting in trees, much like
modern treeswifts and hummingbirds.

Survival tactics

Nicola S. Clayton

There are around 11,000 species of birds known to exist today, from the miniscule Bee Hummingbird that buzzes like a bee and weighs no more than an acorn, to the majestic Wandering Albatross that has the largest wingspan of any bird. In general, birds are light for their size. Even the tallest and heaviest living bird species, the flightless ostrich, may grow to be almost 3 metres (9 feet) tall but weighs less than 160 kilogrammes (353 pounds). The avian world is filled with diversity, reflecting the ways that different bird species have adapted to survive the trials and tribulations of life in their own unique ways. Look at the sheer variety of the beaks of Darwin's finches that live on the Galápagos islands, so exquisitely attuned in size and shape to the foods that they eat.

Birds and their dinosaur cousins are more recently evolved than mammals. A limited number of birds survived the dinosaur disaster, but then rapidly evolved diverse body plans – some large, some small, but all with hollow bones, a lack of teeth and for the most part glorious wings, all of which are adaptations promoting their motoric skills in the air, as well as on the land and in water. Consider a murmuration of starlings as they manoeuvre through the sky – like a corps de ballet performance of *Swan Lake* – in order to distract and evade potential predators; or the complex social interactions of rooks and jackdaws, which can be found in swirls of 55,000 or more as they prepare to roost, communicating both visually and acoustically as they jostle for position, negotiating both individually and collectively the perfect night-time place to rest. A swirl of black bodies is well concealed against the night's sky, but there are many other ways birds can disguise themselves

The Nicobar Pigeon, *Caloenas nicobarica*, is the closest living relative of the extinct Dodo, *Raphus cucullatus*. Recently, one was found in northwest Australia, far from its usual Indonesian range. Such vagrant travellers reveal how the Dodo's ancestors reached Mauritius, but also give us clues about how birds might change their ranges in response to climate change.

in daylight too. Some species use camouflage to blend into the background, for example the Tawny Frogmouth that perches on a tree in such a way that it simply looks like part of the bark. Other species rely on disappearance in pure sight, akin to black art magic. The Orange Fruit Dove that lives on the island of Taveuni, Fiji and the Guianan Cock-of the-rock from Brazil and other regions of South America possess feathers that are the natural complement of the dark green leaves on the lush island, and therefore are completely concealed in the undergrowth. They only become conspicuous when the male reveals his true colours to a female, out in the open, with his elaborate mating display.

The word 'evolution' means change and, to survive in a
turbulent world, all life has to continue to accommodate
environmental challenges as they ebb and flow through time
and space, especially birds that encounter multiple habitats.
Perhaps the most stunning example is that of migratory birds
such as the nimble Arctic Tern, which makes a round trip of about
80,500 kilometres (50,000 miles) a year between the Arctic and
Antarctica, and back again once their chicks have fledged.
They have to cope with changing conditions in their environment
and climate, and circumnavigate all the ensuing challenges in
finding limited resources such as food, shelter and opportunities
for breeding.

Some birds go to great lengths to deploy mental as well as
physical adaptations. For nine months a year birds-of-paradise
and manakins spend up to 90% of their time practising and
performing courtship dances to woo their avian partners, and
rehearsal is key. It can take around eight years to master the dance
and a further four years to become an expert, not that far removed
from the intense training required for a human professional
dancer. Such learning requires both mind and body memory,
remembering all the procedural skills to enact the appropriate
twirl and experiential memories of what is required, when, and
for who.

Perhaps the masters of combining mental and physical
adaptations are the corvids, for these birds remember what
they have hidden where and when, and they use their memories
to plan ahead, taking account of what others may be thinking.
They go to great lengths to protect their stashes of hidden food
from onlookers, deploying tactics akin to those magicians use to
minimize the chance that others might steal from them. Some
species, such as Clark's Nutcrackers, have enlarged throat patches
to conceal and carry huge amounts of food until they have the
chance to stash it. They have adjusted to the latest changes in
their environment, becoming increasingly urban, eating food
that humans have discarded in waste bins on motorway service
stations. No wonder they are termed 'feathered apes', with brains
that are – relative to body size – as large as chimpanzees.

Eurasian Jays, *Garrulus glandarius,* hide food to eat in the winter. If they are seen by potential pilferers as they cache, jays that have been thieves themselves re-hide those caches.

The sheer diversity of manners and movements, physical traits and mental tactics deployed in the avian kingdom is stunning, not just as seen in their current forms in the 21st century, but over evolutionary time and space. That's where we can observe the true dynamics of those avian adaptations that have led to our current bird survivors. Where next? What will the future hold?

Labels in image: Collocalia nidifica / Isles adjoining Junk Ceylon / MUS. / BRIT. / CLASS III. / B. Food Products. / BM Nest Reg N.78 1-2 / Edible Bird's-nests (1st sort) / Collocalia nidifica. / Isles adjoining / Junk Ceylon. / No.4158

Nest of White-nest Swiftlet
Aerodramus fuciphagus

Famous as the key ingredient in the delicacy 'bird's nest soup' prized in Chinese cuisine, these dainty nests are made entirely of hardened saliva. White-nest Swiftlets breed in large colonies inside caves where they have solved the problem of gathering nesting material by using their spit to create the nest instead. Squeezing out sticky saliva from a gland under their tongues, they create the cups directly onto cave walls, strand by strand, over several weeks. The nests become glued to the rock as they dry. Such white nests are highly valued, so in recent years a new industry has developed across Southeast Asia to encourage swiftlets to breed in specially constructed buildings, where the nests can be easily harvested. However, demand for premium 'cave fresh' nests by collectors is still high, placing pressure on the wild colonies.

Common Murre eggs
Uria aalge

The Common Murre, also known as the Common Guillemot, lays the most variable-coloured eggs of any bird species. This medium-sized auk breeds in colonies on coastal cliffs where thousands of nesting birds pack together almost shoulder to shoulder, each pair's single egg laid directly onto rock ledges. The unique appearance of each egg helps parents identify their own egg amongst the bustling colony. On sloping cliff shelves, the adults brood their eggs facing upslope with the pointed end between their legs facing downslope. Recent research suggests that their pointed shape helps to makes the egg more stable on sloping ledges, making them easier for adults to move about but preventing them from rolling away.

Rook nest
Corvus frugilegus

Rooks nest together in trees, building their bulky stick nests just a few metres apart in colonies called rookeries. Nests are often used for many years, so may become large structures as the adults repair and refresh them each year. Usually starting in February, adults can be spotted carrying surprisingly large sticks to their chosen nest site, adding broken off twigs from the trees around them and also frequently stealing materials from neighbours' nests. Finally, the wide stable nest is lined with dried grasses and dead leaves and may also include human-made materials such as coloured plastic-fibre strings, commonly known as baler twine and found on farms where rooks forage.

Giant Elephant Bird egg
Aepyornis maximus

Unique to the island of Madagascar and amongst the largest birds in the world, reaching up to 3 metres (10 feet) tall and weighing in at 700 kilogrammes (1,553 pounds), elephant birds became extinct around 1,000 years ago, not long after the arrival of humans on the island. Despite their relatively recent disappearance, their skeletal fossil record is patchy, as bones don't survive well in Madagascar's hot and humid climate. Eggshell remains are far more common, including the largest known eggs of any bird or dinosaur. Eggshells also preserve DNA better than bone, enabling researchers to crack the elephant bird family tree. Molecular analysis of fragments gathered from across the whole island, with the support of local fieldworkers, has confirmed just three species of elephant bird. However, unexpected genetic diversity found in fragments from the north, where no skeletons have yet been found, is evidence of a different lineage which may prove to be another species.

Azure-crowned Hummingbird (adults, juveniles and nest)
Saucerottia cyanocephala

The Victorians were fascinated by hummingbirds, entranced by their tiny size and glittering colours. The ornithologist John Gould staged a public display of his extensive hummingbird collection during the Great Exhibition of 1851 in London. Visitors could see hundreds of specimens like these set up in cases with real and artificial plants, in an effort to make them appear life-like. This little group of adults around chicks in a nest, from one of Gould's cases, is a typical example of his approach, but isn't a true likeness of hummingbird behaviour. These hummingbirds are in fact mostly solitary and, after mating, only the female incubates the egg and raises the chicks. Females also build the delicate nests, using flakes of lichen, plant fibres, strands of spiderweb and the fluffy hairs from airborne seeds.

Nest of Guam Flycatcher
Myiagra frecycineti

Historically on the Pacific island of Guam, forests rang with songs of some 14 species of birds, including several endemics. Following the accidental introduction of the brown tree snake, some time between 1944 and 1952, to the formerly snake-free island, the forests fell silent. Most likely arriving amongst US military cargo, the snake wiped out native birds, eating eggs and young of ground and tree-nesting species alike. By the 1980s, ten forest species had disappeared from Guam. Two species became extinct and another two species extinct in the wild, surviving only in captivity. This nest was built by the endemic Guam Flycatcher, a small boldly marked bird known in the local CHamora language as CHuguangguang. It was still common in some areas in the 1970s but plummeted to extinction in 1983. Brown tree snakes continue to pose a threat, with a new population found on Cocos Island, a key reserve for the reintroduced critically endangered Guam Rail or Ko'ko, in 2020.

Common Cuckoo and eggs
Cuculus canorus

The migratory Common Cuckoo is widespread across Europe and Asia, where males announce themselves to females with their bold 'cuckoo' calls when they arrive in breeding territories in the spring. They are brood parasites, with the females laying an egg into the nest of another species, where the chick will be looked after by its unsuspecting foster carers. How the females manage this was revealed in the early 1920s by the detailed research of ornithologist Edgar Chance who, combining careful observation of individual females and collecting their eggs and the host clutches, discovered that each female monitors some ten or more nests, waiting until each host has finished laying a clutch and leaves the nest unguarded. The cuckoo then flies into the nest, removes an egg and replaces it with her own. Chance filmed this, revealing that the switch is completed in under ten seconds. It has been illegal to take most wild birds' eggs since 1954; however, historic collections such as Chance's remain important in modern research.

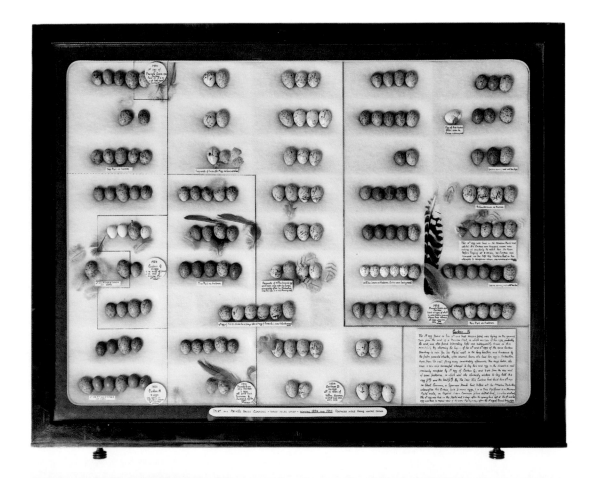

Great albatross chick
Diomedea

The so-called great albatrosses, including Wandering and Antipodean Albatrosses have the widest wingspans in the world, reaching some 3.5 metres (11½ feet) in the largest Wanderers. They typically breed every two years, with pairs attempting to raise just one chick per season. Chicks are left for days at a time in the breeding colonies, while their parents make foraging flights of thousands of kilometres. At sea, the greatest threat albatrosses face is death by collision or entanglement in fishing gear, such as the baited hooks of longline vessels. The risk of albatross bycatch can be readily mitigated with a range of measures, such as the 'Hookpod' system, which automatically releases baited hooks at a safe depth. Working with the Albatross Task Force since 2006, fisheries in South Africa have reduced their bycatch rate by 99% using various approaches; many other global fisheries are also successfully reducing their rates. However, with 15 of the 22 species of albatross threatened with extinction, the co-operation of even more international fisheries is crucial to their survival.

Common Hoopoe
Upupa epops

A long beak, striking plumage and jaunty crest give the Common Hoopoe a distinctive appearance. However, one of its most interesting features is less visible. The species has an unusually large preen gland, located just above the base of the tail feathers. In most birds this produces the oils used to help keep their plumage in good condition. Female hoopoes pack some extra punch into their oil, producing a unique, dark, foul-smelling secretion full of bacteria. Using this for preening themselves to help repel nest parasites, they also paint it on their eggs, staining the blue-green shells brown. The pungent liquid has antibiotic properties and is absorbed by special microscopic pits in the eggshells to help protect the developing embryos from infection.

Australian Zebra Finch
Taeniopygia castanotis

Popular as a caged bird, it's easy to forget that in the wild these striking little finches are tough survivors, capable of enduring the arid bush habitats of their native Australia where temperatures can reach over 40°C (104°F). During the final days of incubation, adult finches sing a special 'heat call' song to their eggs when temperatures rise above 26°C (79°F). The song causes the energy-generating mitochondria inside the embryos'

cells to produce less heat, helping to protect the unhatched young from overheating. The effects of this sonic cell programming appear to last after hatching. Chicks in hotter sunny nests develop more slowly than those from cooler shady nests, and they also reach a smaller size when fully grown. It's thought that the smaller body size helps the young birds cope better with managing extreme temperatures in their challenging environment.

Great Hornbill
Buceros bicornis

After mating, female Great Hornbills settle
into their nest, usually a natural hole in a
large forest tree that they seal up using their
own droppings to leave just a small opening.
Behind the hardened wall, the female can look
after her eggs and young, safe from predators
but entirely dependent on the male for food.
After hatching, the male brings up to 185 food
items a day to the nest, mainly fruit but also
large insects and small vertebrates. The female
breaks out of the walled nest a few weeks
before the chicks fledge, but the young birds
seal the entrance again, so staying protected
while both adults feed them until they are
strong enough to break out themselves.

Palm Cockatoo
Probosciger aterrimus

The largest cockatoos in the world, Palm
Cockatoos are also known as the only non-
human species to make a tool for drumming.
Males break off sticks, then trim them with their
powerful beaks to shape their ideal drumstick.
Using their stick, or sometimes a seedpod,
they drum on hollow branches, especially
when a female is around, sometimes going
for more than a minute. Analysis of over 130
drum solos by 18 males has revealed that the
cockatoos have a strong sense of rhythm, with
individuals showing their own signature styles.
The appreciation of a good rhythm by these
cockatoos may help us understand how
a preference for beats also evolved
in humans.

Macaroni Penguin
Eudyptes chrysolophus

Same-sex pairings are well known amongst many penguin species in captivity, including Macaroni Penguins. Pairs mark their bonds with courtship displays to each other, which in Macaroni Penguins includes preening each other – known as allopreening. Same sex courtship displays are also common amongst wild penguins. In one study of King Penguins nearly 29% of the displaying pairs studied at random were same sex, confirmed by DNA samples obtained afterwards. Though some pairs clearly showed bonded behaviours, this study suggested that wild pairs rarely raise young, needing an egg to look after. By contrast, many strongly bonded captive penguin pairs that have been given an egg by their keepers, have hatched and raised chicks very successfully.

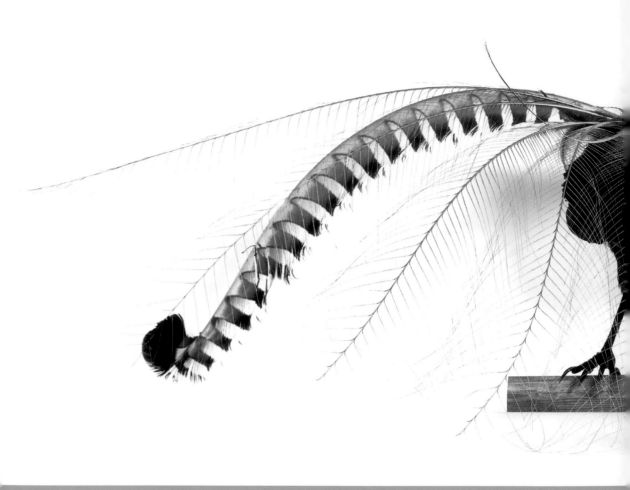

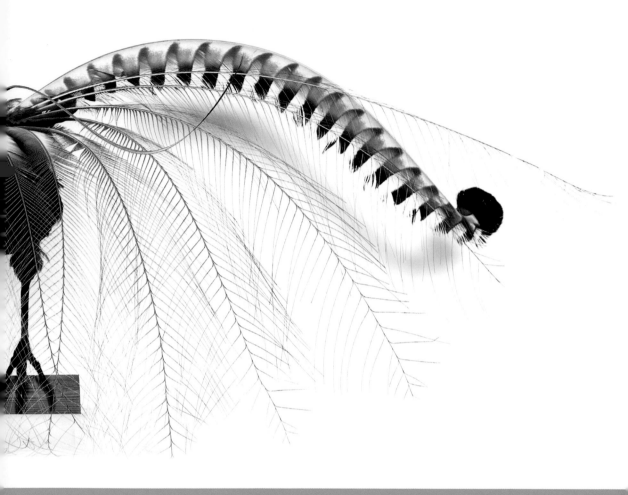

Superb Lyrebird
Menura novaehollandiae

Male Superb Lyrebirds really do make a big song and dance about courtship. They prepare several mounds of bare dirt in their territory so, if they encounter a female, they can launch an elaborate performance on the nearest mound to attract her. They start a dance routine by vibrating their fanned tail and beating their wings, but it's the loud, complex song that is key. Males are incredible mimics, with up to 80% of their song featuring detailed imitations of other birds' calls. Over 20 other species have been recorded, and other animal or human sounds might also be repeated. The quality of the song tells females about the age and condition of a possible mate; males with a wider range and accuracy of mimic songs have a better chance of winning the female vote.

Great Tit
Parus major

Winter means tougher times foraging for many species. Great Tits are highly intelligent, opportunistic and have complex social networks, meaning that they can develop innovative behaviour under pressure and also pass on what they learn. An extreme example comes from caves in Hungary, where Great Tits can be found systematically hunting for hibernating pipistrelle bats when other food becomes scarce. The tits search for bats, sometimes homing in on the calls made by bats waking up. Once a victim is found and caught, the tits peck at them with their robust pointed beaks, eating brains, organs and muscles. Bat hunting has been observed for over 10 years now, suggesting that the behaviour is not only passed between individuals, but also down the generations.

Eurasian Blackcap
Sylvia atricapilla

These small migratory warblers are sometimes called 'northern nightingales' thanks to their loud, fluting spring songs. Males arriving back to their breeding grounds set up their territories in mixed woodlands or bushy hedges, and mark out their patch by singing to advertise to incoming females. As well as the fruity main song, male Eurasian blackcaps also have a second song, described as a chatty, fizzy twittering, which they sing all year round. This quieter song is also used by females and young birds, seeming to be for shorter distance communication than the males' bold far-carrying main song.

Blue Bird-of-Paradise
(male and female)
Paradisaea rudolphi

The 42 species of birds-of-paradise show an extraordinary diversity of colour, plumage, displays and calls, all used by the males to attract females and prove their fitness as a potential mate. A team of researchers using museum specimens, together with sound and video recordings, have discovered that species with the most complex colours also have the most complex vocal performances.

The Blue Bird-of-Paradise is one of these, with the males revealing a shimmering spectrum of blue and purple shades as he hangs upside down vibrating his plumes. At the height of his efforts, his twanging calls can shift into a rhythmic, almost electronic buzzing. If the female moves away, he tries to lure her back with urgent chittering and chattering.

DAZZLING DISPLAYS

Raggiana Bird-of-Paradise (male) *Paradisaea raggiana*
King Bird-of-Paradise (male) *Cicinnurus regius*

Birds-of-paradise hold an enduring fascination for humans across time and cultures. Europeans found out about them from specimens traded from Indonesia into Europe but, lacking knowledge of birds in life, naturalists guessed at how the birds might use their plumes. Travelling through the islands of Malaysia and Indonesia between 1854–1862, naturalist and explorer Alfred Russel Wallace became the first European to record birds-of-paradise in their home forests and describe their displays. Wallace's explorations were made possible by the assistance of many local guides who helped him find and collect the birds and many other species. The skill and knowledge of local peoples is still crucial today for researchers working with birds-of-paradise, helping to reveal the full complexity of their extraordinary behaviour to the wider world.

King of Saxony Bird-of-Paradise (male)
Pteridophora alberti

The long plumes, resembling strings of flags, of the male King of Saxony Bird-of-Paradise are unique amongst birds. Set along a bare feather shaft, each flag is flat and filmy, with its upper surface a bright glossy sky-blue, almost appearing enamelled. Males move the plumes around during their displays, raising them and bringing them forwards over their heads. They often start with a simple display, perched high in the canopy, singing and mouth-gaping with a little plume waving. After a visiting female shows interest, the male launches into a full display, shifting down to a lower level to perform his 'understorey bouncing display' – singing, puffed up, bouncing the branch up and down and sweeping his plumes about so that they catch the light amongst the forest shadows.

Anna's Hummingbird (male)
Calypte anna

Since the 1960s, these tiny sparkling hummingbirds have extended their range from California northwards along the Pacific coast slope to British Columbia and beyond, with regular sightings in southeastern Alaska! Taking advantage of nectar from introduced plants such as Blue Gum, *Eucalpytus globulus,* and helped by garden hummingbird feeders, they have also proved capable of surviving freezing winter temperatures. To power their flight, hummingbirds typically have very high metabolic rates, processing their sugary diet into the energy needed for their muscles. In cold temperatures, these hummers also convert sugars to fat reserves during the day and, to save energy, can slow their heart rate, drop body temperature and enter torpor. Motionless, fluffed up with eyes closed, they seem frozen until rising temperatures rouse them, coming fully awake in only minutes.

Trade skin of Raggiana Bird-of-Paradise
Paradisaea raggiana

In the 1500s, traditionally prepared skins were the first evidence Europeans encountered of fabulously plumed birds from Indonesia and New Guinea. Dried, with legs and feet removed, these so-called 'trade skins' led to a belief in the West that the birds floated in the air, sipping dew, until they died and fell to Earth. They became known as birds-of-paradise and their skins were highly desirable, first for study but then for fashion, especially for decorating hats. By the early 1900s up to 80,000 skins were being exported annually to European auction houses, until the trade was ended in the 1920s by import bans. In their New Guinea home ranges, birds-of-paradise have been important to Indigenous peoples for thousands of years, with

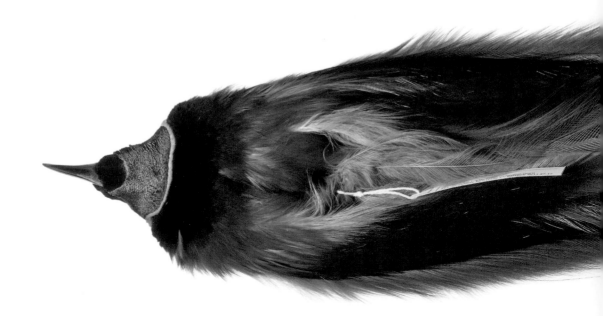

some plumes being specially selected for use in ceremonial head-dresses. Working to protect both culture and birds, community conservation projects help to preserve head-dresses, keeping them in use for as long as possible to reduce the demand for harvesting new feathers.

Ruff
Calidris pugnax

Closely related to sandpipers, Ruffs are migratory waders of shallow wetlands, swampy meadows and marshy tundra. They are named for the breeding plumage of the males, which sport a broad ruff, ear tufts and facial wattles to help impress females. This plumage differs enormously between individuals, with over 800 variations recorded by one study. Males perform in group leks, raising their tufts, spreading their ruffs (bottom left), posturing and fighting to hold the best patches and attract visiting females (bottom right). However, some rare males do without the finery and displays, having a more female-like plumage (top). Known as faeders, less than 1% of males inherit this look, which enables them to move unchallenged amongst displaying males and gain access to females.

Great Bustard (female and male)
Otis tarda

Male Great Bustards are amongst the largest flying birds in the world and are renowned for their complex display behaviour during the breeding season. Living in open grasslands, the normally well-camouflaged males reveal themselves in a flamboyant display, appearing to turn themselves inside out into a shining white beacon of feathers. Females consider their mate choice carefully, using age, weight and display effort to help identify an ideal candidate. An

essential part of their decision lies in a detailed inspection of a prospective mate's cloaca, prominent under his raised tail. Going so far as to peck at the opening, females seem to be checking for signs of parasites or diseases. Males boost their health for this examination by eating toxic blister beetles in spring. The beetles contain potentially lethal cantharidin which, eaten in the right amount, acts as self-medication against parasitic and bacterial infections.

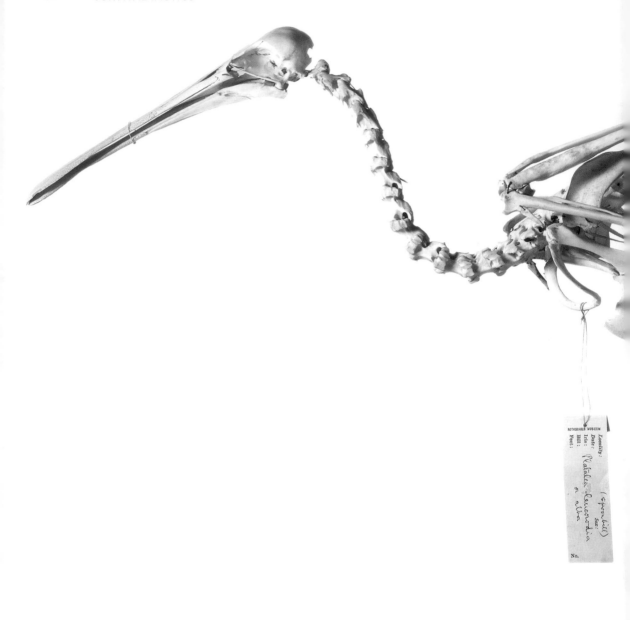

Spoonbill skeleton
Platalea

Far from being clumsy, the wide-tipped bill of the six spoonbill species is a highly specialized, precision tool. Wading through shallow water, spoonbills search for prey such as shrimp and small fish by sweeping their slightly open bill from side to side. Its flattened shape helps the beak move efficiently through the water, while clusters of sensitive nerve receptors in the bill detect when food is touched, allowing the spoonbill to snap up a snack without needing to see it. The density of the touch receptors can be measured by the distribution of the tiny pits that are visible in the bone of the bill. It is through these pits that the receptors connect to the nervous system. The higher the number of pits, the greater the sensitivity in that area. In spoonbills, the highest densities are along the edges and insides of the beak.

Common Barn-owl
Tyto alba

Owls need to pinpoint their prey horizontally to find it, then vertically to know how far to swoop down on it. Barn-owls have very light sensitive vision but are able to hunt in total darkness thanks to their extraordinary hearing. The shape of the feathered facial disk acts as a pair of sound reflectors to gather and direct noises to the ears. To achieve the precision for hunting, the ears are set at slightly different levels on each side of the head and are slightly different shapes. The right ear is cupped upwards and the left cupped downwards, making each ear more sensitive to noises coming from different directions; the owl's brain can process the tiny differences between sounds from each ear to give it the location of its target.

Eurasian Blue Tit
(adult and juvenile)
Cyanistes caeruleus

To the human eye, male and female Eurasian
Blue Tits appear virtually identical. However, it's
very different for the birds themselves, as their
vision is sensitive to ultraviolet wavelengths
reflected by their plumage. The upperside of
the tail, back, blue-black back of the neck and
white crown all appear different in males and
females, but it's the blue crest which stands out
the most between the sexes. Humans can see a
hint of shiny blue, but it's a shadow of what the
microscopic structure of the plumage reflects
to blue tits. After moulting out of duller juvenile
colours, both sexes have bright crests, the males'
crest being much brighter than the females'.
Researchers have found both males and females
prefer mates with brighter crests as it is an
indication of fitness.

Manx Shearwater
Puffinus puffinus

Along with petrels and albatrosses, shearwaters are known as tubenoses, thanks to the elongated structure of their nostrils. These ocean wanderers solve the challenge of finding food in the open seas by using their keen sense of smell, aided by an enlarged olfactory lobe (the part of the brain involved in smell). Shearwaters can pick up scents of potential food drifting on the winds across the ever-moving surface of the sea. In particular, they are very receptive to the stinky chemical dimethyl sulphide released by certain types of plankton and also respond to fish oils, often dispersed by other seabirds feeding on a shoal. Once detected, shearwaters fly zig-zag upwind to track the source down, which could be over a kilometre away.

Eurasian Jay
Garrulus glandarius

Jays are usually omnivores, but in autumn collecting acorns for winter food stores becomes their priority. These bright woodland birds visit oak trees to gather ripe acorns, tucking up to nine into a throat pouch before flying away to save them for later by burying or hiding them under leaves and moss. A single bird can cache over 5,500 acorns in a single season, often over a kilometre from the source tree. Although jays return to find and eat them during winter, many acorns are left over, allowing a new generation of oak trees to sprout in the spring. This ancient relationship between birds and trees helps old woodland regenerate, but also helps plant entirely new woodland, making jays a valuable conservation ally.

Common Raven
Corvus corax

The intelligence of crows and ravens is recognized in mythology and folklore worldwide. In Norse mythology, the god Odin was kept informed about the world by his two ravens, Huginn 'Thought' and Muninn 'Memory'. Researchers working with captive ravens today continue to discover the complexity of their cognition, finding out that at only four months old young ravens are on a problem-solving par with adult great apes. A modern captive Hugin even proved capable of deceiving his dominant male companion Munin in food-retrieving experiments. Better at finding the food rewards concealed in some, but not all, clusters of canisters, subordinate Hugin kept losing out to Munin scrounging off him. Hugin started pretending to eat from empty canisters, distracting Munin away from reward canisters which Hugin then quickly flew to for a head start on the treats inside. Hugin was clearly misleading his companion, but after some days Munin got wise to it and eventually starting opening boxes for himself.

Spix's Macaw
Cyanopsitta spixii

Parrots are one of the most threatened groups of birds in the world, impacted by habitat loss and trade. In 2019, Spix's Macaw was classed as extinct in the wild, with a population of about 180 surviving only in captivity. Observations of the captive birds have revealed complex behaviour, recording over 35 different actions and displays that help these very social birds communicate.

One striking pose is a distracting death display used by young birds when stressed or approached by a possible predator – they fall motionless onto their backs, even reducing their breathing to add to the illusion. A small flock of these stunning little macaws were released into their Brazilian home range in 2022 in the hope of re-establishing the species in the wild.

Kagu
Rhynochetus jubatus

The only species in its taxonomic family, the flightless Kagu is endemic to the island of New Caledonia in the South Pacific. It is, like many other flightless island endemics, unfortunately endangered, in this case impacted by the predation of dogs intruding on its forest homelands. Kagu pairs are territorial and often develop long term bonds. They lay a single egg in a simple nest on the ground, taking turns to incubate. Successfully raising a chick though is not just down to the parents. Young birds can stay in their parents' territory for up to six years before moving on to breed themselves – as many as five might be hanging around. While these older offspring don't help to feed the chick, they do help to defend the home range and their presence is linked to a better chance of the chick being reared successfully.

Northern Gannet
Morus bassanus

Plunge-diving is a highly specialized hunting method used by a number of bird species. Gannets take it to the extreme, diving from up to 45 metres (148 feet) high at speeds of more than 20 metres per second (48 miles per hour) to take fish by surprise underwater. Birds might make as many as 100 dives on one trip; the impact of even one dive could potentially be fatal, so the sleek form and feathers of these dynamic hunters reveal many adaptations. In a dive, the arrow-like shape of the beak cleanly pierces the water, then special muscles behind the skull bunch to stop the slender neck buckling. As the upper chest strikes the sea surface, the force of impact is spread out by the densely packed contour feathers.

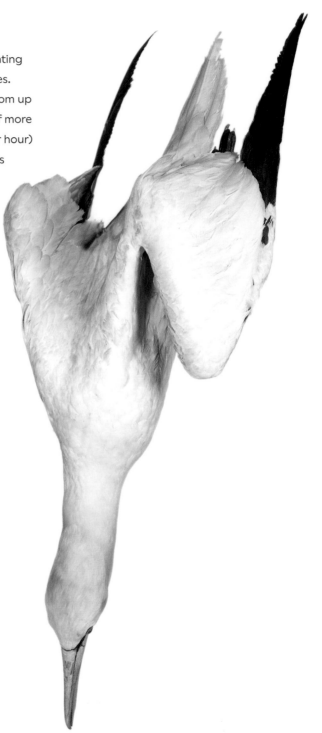

Common Kestrel (female) and Eurasian Bullfinch (male)
Falco tinnunculus and *Pyrrhula pyrrhula*

Shy bullfinches need the cover of thickets and scrub to hide, nest and forage in, safe away from the sharp eyes of predators such as kestrels and sparrowhawks. In open farmland hedges are a vital substitute for lost scrub and woodland and help to link up remaining patches, providing habitat for thousands of vertebrate and invertebrate species. Over 50% of UK hedgerows were removed between 1947 and 2007, and around 60% of what remains is not in good condition. Many declining 'farmland' birds are woodland and scrub birds pushed to the hedge; over 80% of UK woodland bird species can be found in hedgerows, highlighting their importance. Fortunately, hedgerows are now a protected priority habitat, with their conservation and regeneration offering life support to birds across rural, garden and even urban areas.

Common Kestrel
with a

Southern Cassowary
Casuarius casuarius

Only 60 flightless bird species survive today, such as this Southern Cassowary. Flightless species were more common in the past; over 160 flightless species have gone extinct since the Late Pleistocene 126,00 years ago. Flightless birds are more likely to go extinct than flying species, being particularly vulnerable to human influences, such as hunting or introduced predator species. Cassowaries are shy forest residents, but as they lose habitat to human development and forests are split by roads, they come increasingly into contact and conflict with people. Being large, potentially aggressive and armed with hard heads and long claws, they have a bad reputation. But most attacks are linked to humans feeding them, encouraging them to become bolder. Far more cassowaries are harmed by human impacts than vice-versa – collisions with cars and dog attacks are both major causes of death.

CAS. C. VIOLICOLLIS
B.M. REG. 1939 12 9-B86

Himalayan Monal
Lophophorus impejanus

Seasonal migrations can also be altitudinal, where birds in mountainous habitats move up and down slopes tracking optimal temperatures and food opportunities. The Himalayan Monal is believed to make the greatest altitudinal movement of all the Himalayan pheasants, in parts of its range spending summer above 4,300 metres (14,100 feet) and coming down in winter to below 3,200 metres (10,500 feet). Researchers in the region are concerned that, as climate warms, Himalayan Monal and other pheasants will be pushed to higher altitudes as their lower ranges shrink. While the Himalayan Monal is still relatively common, some Himalayan pheasants are already rare. Conservationists are warning that new areas of possible habitat should be identified and protected now, in case populations of these pheasants have to be translocated to new reserves in the future.

European Robin
Erithacus rubecula

Thanks to their confident behaviour around people and a rich history of folklore, the bright-chested European Robin is a UK national favourite. They are strong singers, with their clear silvery whistling a familiar sound across parks, gardens and woodland. Unusually for a UK species, robins sing all year round, changing their song with the seasons. In spring, males stake out and defend their territories with bold, flowing, high-pitched notes. After the breeding season, in autumn, the song becomes quieter and sounds almost melancholic. It's still a song to hold territory, but in winter both sexes establish a patch so both now sing. Robins are often among the first to be heard in the dawn chorus and will sing into the evening too. In urban areas, they can also often be heard at night, triggered into song by artificial lighting.

Eurasian Nightjar
Caprimulgus europaeus

Beautifully camouflaged for hiding during the day, this nightjar species is mainly nocturnal, both in its summer breeding grounds and during its migration to its winter ranges. Researchers using tiny data-loggers, attached to adult nightjars during their autumn migrations between Europe and Africa, have discovered they use different tactics for travelling through different habitats. They relax passing through hospitable terrain, flying shorter distances and pausing to feed. Faced with hostile conditions, such as deserts or sea crossings, they rush, flying further, faster and higher. Adjusting altitude on longer flights is crucial to help them gain speed, using less energy by reaching levels of reduced air density and less turbulence for a smoother passage.

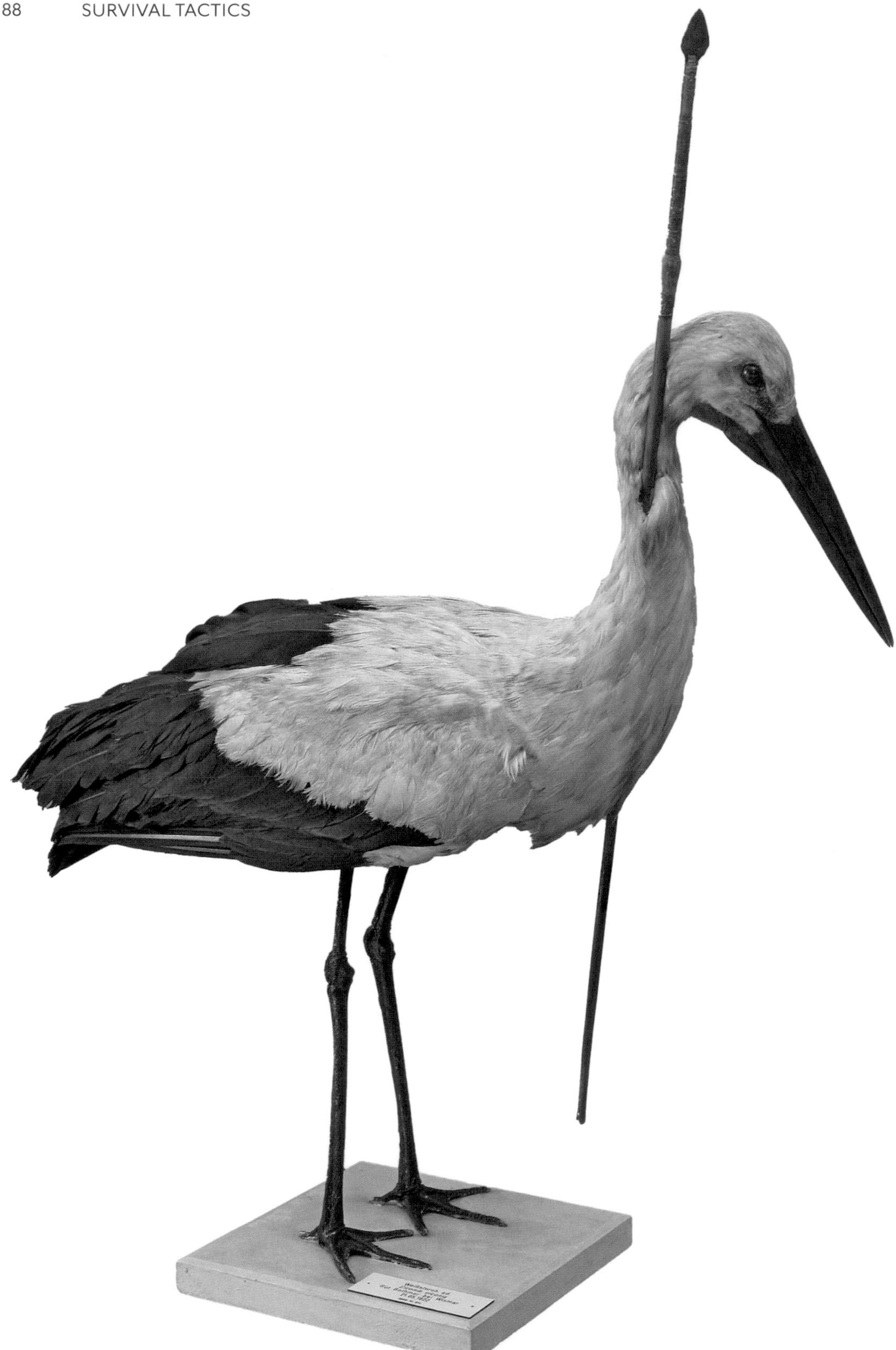

White Stork
Ciconia ciconia 'Pfeilstorch'

In spring 1822, a White Stork was shot near the German village of Klütz; a normal looking adult but carrying a 75 cm (29½ in) long arrow in its neck. Examination of the arrow revealed that the bird had come from Africa, flying some 3,220 km (2,000 miles) north having survived the strike. For over a century, naturalists had been baffled by the mystery of why some birds appeared and disappeared every year. Hibernation was a popular explanation, but the hard evidence of the stork's travel was crucial proof that birds simply moved to different places for different seasons. Known as Pfeilstörche (arrow storks), some 25 storks carrying arrows or spears have now been recorded in Europe. This fragile specimen was the very first to be collected and is preserved in the collection of the University of Rostock, Germany where it serves to share this remarkable story.

Birds of
the future

Mary Colwell

As I write, both the cawing of Carrion Crows and the indignant wails of Herring Gulls join the cooing of city pigeons as the dominant morning soundscape around my home in Bristol, England. I enjoy hearing them, they are characterful chancers that slot easily into this world of buildings and traffic, and in a nature-depleted country I will take what I can get. Bristolians are so used to them now they barely register. Their familiarity, though, belies a disturbing trend for the future of wildlife on Earth.

Crows and gulls are 'generalists' that adapt well to a world dominated by humans – they eat a varied diet of their natural food (carrion, live prey and vegetable matter) as well as that supplied by our wasteful littering habits, and they can nest in our highly modified landscapes – a Herring Gull is as at home on the roof of a block of flats as on a sea cliff; a Carrion Crow can nest in ancient woodland as well as a city park. But this is not the case for many other species. The specialists of this world can only thrive in specific landscapes and on certain wild food – think Turtle Doves, Tree Sparrows, Capercaillie and Nightingales for example. The natural world around us is switching from variety and diversity to a cohort dominated by canny generalists who can turn their wing or beak to most situations. This is an entirely human-made situation, and we are waking up to the enormity of it all.

As the 20th century drew to a close, the rose-tinted view of the Earth as a gift that keeps on giving, a position we have held with certainty for generations, rapidly disintegrated. The new era is bathed in the clearer, harder light of reality, and a realization that nothing is infinite except our desire for more. For thousands of

The bubbling call of the Eurasian Curlew, *Numenius arquata*, is an iconic sound of UK uplands, but this red-listed species is rapidly declining. Securing the future of this species and many others depends on us changing how we use and manage habitats to better support all wildlife.

years, we have assumed the planet was resilient and that it would always provide for our ever-increasing needs. Natural resources, both living and inanimate, were there for the taking, and take we did, unleashing the potential for unprecedented growth. The agrarian and industrial ages released us from the vagaries of depending on a wild, uncontrollable, shifting planet. Humanity staked its claim as the dominant species on Earth and drove its flag into the earth with the confidence that the future could only get better. Over the last few decades, however, it is increasingly hard to ignore the fact that this complex human-made web is fraying and unravelling. Where we once saw abundance, we now

Thousands of Common Kingfishers, *Alcedo atthis*, were once killed every year for the trade in fashionable feathers. Benefitting in more recent times from improvements in water quality and the creation of new wetland habitats, their plumage is now more familiar as a bright blue flash flying rapidly along a river.

see depletion and exhaustion, where we assumed resilience, we find fragility, and even the Earth's climate is changing alarmingly in response to our actions, impacting all of life. We are being challenged to see an entirely different scenario for the future, one that demands that we change course.

The effect on wildlife of the transformation of the planet has been a shift away from landscapes full of nuance and diversity to ones dominated by predictability, uniformity and monoculture. We have lost the loveliness and joy of difference, replacing it with a controlled sameness. It is over this subdued planet that the birds fly in beat with the seasons, as they have always done, and through it all they try to find enough space to call home. Some are succeeding, the 'generalists' described above, but many others are failing as we strip away the only conditions in which they thrive. It feels like a hopeless situation, but it isn't, we can make this work better if we really want to.

If we reduced our demands, restored habitats, re-natured landscapes and put health back into the oceans, rivers, soils and forests, this would once again be a singing planet that vibrates to a myriad of voices. If we make this happen, we will rediscover that life-enhancing connection between ourselves and the wild world and we all be so much richer for it. Birds have a unique role to play; they have a special ability to enliven our senses through song, form and colour and they inspire in us an outpouring of creativity in the form of art, poetry, literature and music. Their disappearance is telling us all is not well, and their recovery is a hopeful life-filled sign that we are repairing past damage. Listen to the songs of the world and we will surely make the right choices.

Great Auk egg
Pinguinus impennis

The last known pair of Great Auks were killed in 1844, prized as specimens for collectors. Where hundreds of thousands of these large, flightless seabirds had lived in the North Atlantic and bred on rocky islands from Scotland to Iceland to Canada, only some 80 mounted skins and 80 eggs are now left in collections. Although the desire of collectors led to their final destruction, Great Auks had been systematically over-exploited for centuries, slaughtered on their island colonies for meat, oil and feathers. Taken for granted, the birds were never properly studied by ornithologists until after their extinction. Pairs laid only one egg, incubated on rocky ledges. Eggs are uniquely marked with spots and streaks, and this, known as Spallanzani's Egg after its earliest known owner, is believed to date to the 1760s. It is the oldest dateable egg in the Natural History Museum's collection.

Kaua'i 'Akialoa
Akialoa stejnegeri

The group of birds known as Hawaiian honeycreepers represent both evolutionary triumph and ecological tragedy. From the historical and fossil record over 50 species are known across the Hawaiian islands, all evolving through adaptive radiation from a finch ancestor. Their huge range of beak shapes and sizes developed for nectar feeding, insect catching, wood pecking and foraging styles. The seven known 'Akialoa species had some of the longest beaks, specialized for probing and bark-picking. Following the arrival of humans to the islands about 1,400 years ago, over 30 honeycreepers have become extinct and most remaining ones are endangered. Increasing pressures from habitat loss and the introduction of invasive species, especially mosquitoes spreading avian pox and malaria, caused catastrophic declines. All the 'Akialoa are extinct; the Kaua'i 'Akialoa was the last, seen for a final time in 1969. Many remaining honeycreepers are endangered, and even more threatened now as climate change allows mosquitoes to colonize higher into the mountainous reserves where they live.

CANARIES IN A COAL MINE

Canary resuscitator
Island Canary *Serinus canaria* domestic variety

The saying 'canary in a coal mine' is used to mean something that warns of coming danger, usually by its sensitivity to worsening conditions. It may be a figure of speech, but its origin lies in the long-standing practice of miners taking caged canaries underground as a life-saving safety measure. Because of their high metabolism and need for oxygen, canaries were particularly sensitive to the potentially lethal gases found underground. By keeping an eye on the condition of their captive canaries, miners could monitor for the presence of gases. Introduced into coalmines around 1900, canaries saved many human lives – but often at the cost of their own. The solution was the canary resuscitator, adapted from undersea diving technology. The canary was kept in the compartment with the door open; if it showed signs of gas poisoning, the door could be sealed and oxygen introduced to revive it. While the use of canaries in mines ended in the mid-1980s, the deterioration of many bird species in the world today is an indicator of worsening environmental conditions, both for them and for us. Resuscitating action is needed, but are we heeding the warnings?

Northern Gannet
Morus bassanus

Donated to the research collections in 1939 by the British Trust for Ornithology's Ringing Committee, this juvenile gannet from the Bass Rock in Scotland's Firth of Forth reflects both the importance of this seabird island and also of monitoring over time. The Bass Rock is home to the largest colony of Northern Gannets in the world, numbering over 150,000 in a typical peak season. But in 2022 avian flu reached the colony; footage from CCTV on the island and drone surveys revealed a massive population drop in the previously thronging colony. However, the investigators also spotted that some birds were nesting and bringing up chicks normally. Later, observers noticed some birds with black irises instead of their usual pale blue; blood tests of black-eyed birds revealed them to have antibodies to avian flu, proving they had survived the infection. The 2023 breeding season was encouraging, with the return of more birds than expected, suggesting that the gannets may be starting to cope with the challenge. Only time will tell.

Plastic fragments ingested by Flesh-footed Shearwaters
Ardenna carneipes

Flesh-footed Shearwater chicks should get a diet of fish and squid, but adult birds routinely pick up plastic fragments at sea, which they feed to their young. As the chicks are fed by regurgitation, they cannot avoid the fragments – and they cannot digest them. Filled with plastic instead of food, young birds are effectively starved. They may die in the colonies or, if they manage to regurgitate enough pieces before fledging, may fly away but underweight with reduced chances of survival. A research team called the Adrift Lab has been studying the shearwaters on Lord Howe Island in the Tasmanian Sea, and the multiple impacts of plastics in the marine environment for nearly 20 years. The team recently identified a new disease, plasticosis, the scarring of shearwaters' stomach tissues by the grinding of ingested plastics, which may affect how well nutrients can be absorbed. As more than 1,200 species (including humans) are documented as ingesting plastics, this discovery has major implications.

Leg bones from domestic chicken and Red Junglefowl
Gallus gallus

Chickens were domesticated from the wild Red Junglefowl around 8,000 years ago in Southeast Asia. Originally mainly kept for ritual purposes, chickens became increasingly valued for eggs and meat as they were transported around the world by humans. Chickens are now the most numerous bird on the planet, with a population estimated at well over 30 billion. However, most chickens have a very short lifespan, with commercial broiler chickens raised for meat slaughtered at around six weeks old. Broiler breeds have been selectively developed for rapid growth under intensive farming conditions; the specimens here compare the immature leg bones of a typical slaughter age broiler (left), its foot cut off during butchery, with those of six-week-old (middle) and 35-week-old (right) birds from a hybrid similar to wild Red Junglefowl. The extreme size and growth rate of broilers places so much stress on their bodies, they are effectively unable to survive to maturity.

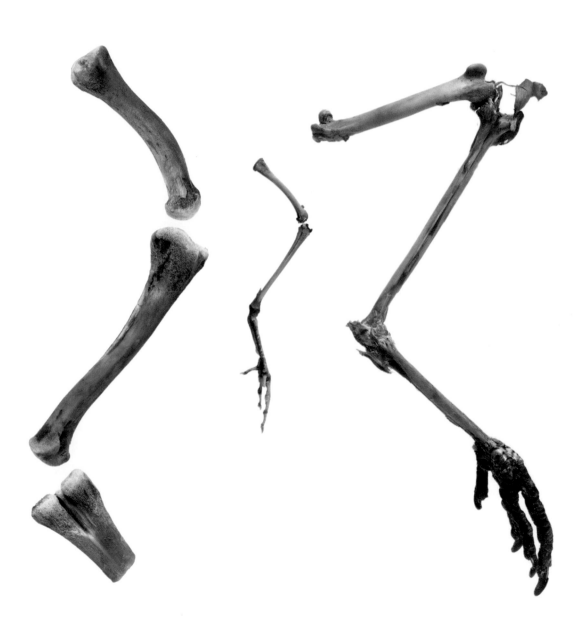

Great White Egret
Ardea alba

Like many egret species, adult Great White Egrets grow long, wispy, ornamental feathers for their breeding season. Seeming to hang off their shoulders in a shimmering robe, such plumes had been prized for decorating hats and headpieces in some parts of the world since the 1600s. However, during the 1870s, in Europe and the USA, a craze for using not just plumes but wings, tails and even whole birds on hats took hold, triggering a lucrative trade for the feathers and skins of many species. With egrets, only the delicate breeding plumes had value so adults were shot and plucked at nesting colonies; carcasses were dumped and any chicks in nests simply left to die. In response to the threat to bird populations from the scale of the slaughter, determined campaigners Emily Williamson and Etta Lemon combined forces to start what became the Royal Society for the Protection of Birds. Their skilful social and political campaigning was further supported by evidence from Natural History Museum scientists of traders' false claims of sustainability. Eventually the Importation of Plumage (Prohibition) Act was passed in 1921, now remembered as a conservation landmark.

Atlantic Puffin
Fratercula arctica

Amongst the best-loved of seabirds, Atlantic Puffins are still common in northern Europe, but the species is now recognized as vulnerable due to rapid declines across most of its European range. Breeding success is being impacted by climate change as sea surface temperatures rise, with the changing temperatures resulting in mismatches in the timing of breeding and prey availability. The results are food shortages, poor chick growth and lower fledging success. Researchers recorded how population crashes in sandeels, a small shoaling fish, in some years led to zero breeding success in the colonies that normally depended on them. Climate change threats to food stocks may be compounded by unsustainable commercial fisheries competing with puffins and other declining seabirds. Concerns about the impact of industrial fishing for sandeels, used in livestock and fish feed, has already led to a ban for UK fishermen in the North Sea, with conservation organizations calling for a restiction on all international sandeel fishing in the UK's seas.

DASHED TO DEATH

Eurasian Sparrowhawk *Accipiter nisus*
European Robin *Erithacus rubecula*
European Goldfinch *Carduelis carduelis*
Dunnock *Prunella modularis*

Window strikes happen when flying birds collide with glass that is invisible to them becaue of surface reflections or its transparency. Although some birds recover from the shock, millions are killed. In the USA, where the problem has been especially well-studied, estimates suggest that between 100 million and 1 billion birds die annually in strikes. Many different species are affected; just a few are represented here by these four specimens. These are all window casualties from the UK donated to the Natural History Museum, London over the past few years and are now part of the research collections. Solutions to making existing glass more visible to birds include marking it with UV–reflecting stickers or films or, in new glass, using permanent patterns of ceramic dots bonded to the surface. Increasingly, legislation is being used to set bird friendly standards for glass in new buildings or renovations.

Philippine Eagle
Pithecophaga jefferyi

One of the world's largest eagles, the
magnificent Philippine Eagle, is also one of its
most critically endangered birds, with probably
less than 250 pairs surviving in a steeply
declining wild population. Found in primary
forest on just four islands in the Philippines,
the eagles are threatened by the clearance of
their forests, with most of the lowland forest
gone and hill and mountain habitats now being
felled. Adults need a large territory to raise
their chicks and, even if successfully fledged,
young birds cannot move safely between forest
fragments to set up new territories. Captive
breeding projects together with community-
led efforts to protect wild nesting sites are
hoping to sustain the species, but without
solving the issue of deforestation, the future
of the Philippine Eagle is precarious.

White-tailed Eagle
Haliaeetus albicilla

Another of the world's largest eagles, the White-tailed Eagle was eradicated in the UK in 1918, when the last surviving female was shot, the sorry end to centuries of persecution by hunting and egg-collecting. They are often called sea-eagles, but research combining place names, historic distribution records and habitat analysis showed that they were actually once widespread across most of the UK, including much of lowland England. Apex predators such as eagles have a crucial role as cornerstone species in ecosystems, helping balance prey populations

and their resources – re-establishing them can therefore be a powerful conservation tool. Reintroduction efforts for White-tailed Eagles started in the UK in 1975, and they are now well-established in parts of Scotland, and successfully breeding in Ireland, with releases being planned for Wales. In July 2023, the first English White-tailed Eagle chick for over 240 years fledged from birds released on the Isle of Wight, raising hopes that these magnificent eagles could once again sweep across their lost lowland haunts.

Biographies

DANIEL J. FIELD is Professor of Vertebrate Palaeontology and Strickland Curator of Ornithology at the University of Cambridge. His research focuses on the evolutionary history of birds and has helped clarify how birds survived and diversified following the mass extinction of non-avian dinosaurs, the evolutionary history of major bird groups, and the evolutionary origins of distinctive features such as the toothless bird skull. He has contributed to the description of several new species of fossil birds, such as the large toothed bird *Janavis finalidens* and the early modern bird *Asteriornis maastrichtensis*, as well as the largest penguin to ever live, *Kumimanu fordycei*.

NICOLA S. CLAYTON is Professor of Comparative Cognition, Department of Psychology, at the University of Cambridge, a Fellow of Clare College, a Fellow of the Royal Society and an Honorary Fellow of the American Ornithological Society. Her expertise lies in the study of comparative cognition, integrating both biology and psychology to introduce new ways of thinking about the evolution and development of intelligence in non-verbal animals, especially corvids, cephalopods, and pre-verbal children. She has a deep passion for birds and has spent most of her academic career studying avian behaviour and cognition, using natural behaviours such as caching, food-sharing, brood parasitism and vocal learning in a variety of songbirds.

MARY COLWELL is Founder and Director of Curlew Action and chair of the Curlew Recovery Partnership England. She is a writer, producer and conservationist, whose 500-mile Curlew Walk across the breadth of Ireland and the UK in 2016 helped raise the profile of the curlew, and led her to write *Curlew Moon*. Mary founded Curlew Action in 2019 to raise awareness about the decline of curlews and to increase engagement with nature through education. She successfully spearheaded the campaign to establish a GCSE in Natural History, which will be available in schools from 2026.

Acknowledgements

With thanks to photographer Lucie Goodayle for superb photography under challenging conditions. Big thanks to the Bird Group at the Natural History Museum Tring in particular the curation team: Mark Adams, Alex Bond, Hein van Grouw, Douglas Russell and Judy White, whose combined expertise and enthusiasm have greatly enriched this exhibition.

Picture credits

p.5 ©Doug Allan/naturepl.com; p.9 ©Phillip Krzeminski; p.15 ©Cast, original specimen in the American Museum of Natural History (AMNHFARB 6515); p.19 Institute of Vertebrate Paleontology and Paleoanthropology (IVPP); p.20 ©Daniel J. Field and Juan Benito; p.26-7 ©Senckenberg; p.31 ©Terry Andrewartha/naturepl.com; p.88 ©Universität Rostock; p.90-1 ©VyacheslavLn/Shutterstock; p.96 ©Museum of Science & Industry/Science & Society Picture Library - All rights reserved; p.99 ©Justin Gilligan (www.justingilligan.com) p.110-111 ©Piotr Krzeslak/Shutterstock.

First published by the Natural History Museum, Cromwell Road, London SW7 5BD
© The Trustees of the Natural History Museum, London, 2024

ISBN 978 0 565 09558 1

A catalogue record for this book is available from the British Library

10 9 8 7 6 5 4 3 2 1

Designed by Bobby Birchall, Bobby&Co.
Reproduction by Saxon Digital Services
Printed by Toppan Leefung Printing Ltd., China